Web Performance in Action

BUILDING FAST WEB PAGES

JEREMY L. WAGNER

MANNING

SHELTER ISLAND

For online information and ordering of this and other Manning books, please visit www.manning.com. The publisher offers discounts on this book when ordered in quantity. For more information, please contact

Special Sales Department
Manning Publications Co.
20 Baldwin Road
PO Box 761
Shelter Island, NY 11964
Email: orders@manning.com

Manning Publications Co.
20 Baldwin Road
PO Box 761
Shelter Island, NY 11964

Development editor:	Susanna Kline
Review editor:	Ivan Martinović
Technical development editor:	Nick Watts
Project editor:	Kevin Sullivan
Copyeditor:	Sharon Wilkey
Proofreader:	Elizabeth Martin
Technical proofreader:	David Fombella Pombal
Typesetter:	Gordan Salinovic
Cover designer:	Marija Tudor

ISBN 9781617293771
Printed in the United States of America
1 2 3 4 5 6 7 8 9 10 – EBM – 21 20 19 18 17 16

brief contents